Carving & Painting an
AMERICAN KESTREL
with Floyd Scholz

Floyd Scholz

Photographs by Tad Merrick

STACKPOLE BOOKS

0 11557 02493 7

For Beatriz

Published by
STACKPOLE BOOKS
5067 Ritter Road
Mechanicsburg, PA 17055
www.stackpolebooks.com

Printed in China

10 9 8 7 6 5 4 3

First edition

Cover design by Wendy Reynolds

All photographs by Tad Merrick unless otherwise credited

Library of Congress Cataloging-in-Publication Data

Scholz, Floyd.
    Carving and painting an American kestrel with Floyd Scholz /
Floyd Scholz; photographs by Tad Merrick.
        p.   cm.
    ISBN 0-8117-2493-X
    1. Wood-carving.   2. Birds in art.   3. American kestrel.   I. Title.
TT199.7 .S37   2003
736'.4—dc21   2002011013

ISBN 978-0-8117-2493-7

Contents

CHAPTER ONE

About the American Kestrel

The American kestrel (*Falco sparverius*) is the Western Hemisphere's smallest and most colorful falcon, and with the exception of the Seychelles kestrel, found on a few isolated islands in the Indian Ocean, it is the smallest falcon found anywhere in the world. Its range extends from the extreme southern tip of the South American continent northward to the rugged treeline of northern Canada and Alaska. *Falco sparverius* exists in at least fifteen recognized subspecies—quite a variety when one considers the extreme variation in habitat and the adaptability this falcon needs, not just to survive, but to thrive in a wide range of climates on a wide variety of prey species.

The American kestrel is a resilient and versatile bird of prey. As is the case with most diurnal (daytime-hunting) birds of prey, the female is noticeably larger and heavier than the male. The commonly held theory regarding this size difference is still a subject of debate among bird experts. It is believed that the female needs a larger body to produce eggs, and a larger mass helps in incubating the eggs and protects the clutch as it develops. Also, a size and strength difference between the sexes allows the pair to catch and kill a much wider range of prey species. In addition to the size difference, the kestrel is the only member of the genus *Falco* found in the Americas in which the sex of an individual can be quickly identified by differing plumage patterns and coloration.The juveniles also differ markedly in plumage patterns and colors. This has been a source of bewilderment for ornithologists who have studied the kestrel. Because they are small, highly active birds, kestrels are able to breed and raise young in their first year. Perhaps the need to distinguish sexual identity begins in the nest.

Kestrels are not fussy when it comes to eating. Their varied diet includes insects (especially grasshoppers), earthworms, small snakes, scorpions, mice, wood rats, and even bats. They will also catch songbirds up to the size of mourning doves if an opportunity presents itself. It's this adaptability and fearlessness that account for the kestrel's wide distribution throughout North, Central, and South America. Even many of the lush tropical islands of the Caribbean have evolved their own unique form of American kestrel. A good example of this is the Cuban form (*Falco s. sparveroides*), which has a great deal more blue plumage on the back and brighter rust coloring on its chest, breast, and belly areas.

With the possible exception of the red-tailed hawk (*Buteo jamaicensis*), the American kestrel is one of the most commonly seen birds of prey in North America. Enhancing this familiarity is the kestrel's ready acceptance of man-made nesting boxes. Kestrels can actually benefit from human development and seem to thrive around farms and suburban environments, most likely due to the concentration of rodents and insects,

RON AUSTING

Aside from a difference in size, the American kestrel is the only North American raptor whose plumage differs dramatically between the sexes. The slate blue coloring of the male wings allows for instant sex recognition.

which are attracted to the artificial light and the easy accessibility of food.

I vividly remember how excited I was when, many years ago, I awoke one spring morning to the piercing *killy, killy, killy* cries of a curious male exploring a recently constructed nest box that was attached to a nearby telephone pole on my property. Needless to say, the local songbird population probably didn't share my enthusiasm. I enjoyed watching the parents as they took turns hunting. The little falcon would course back and forth over the meadow until it spotted something, then hang suspended on frantic wings until just the right moment, when it would drop straight down onto an unsuspecting garter snake or meadow mouse.

Kestrels prefer to live and nest where there is a lot of open terrain, with elevations ranging from sea level to more than 10,000 feet, as long as the environment is not heavily forested. Because they are falcons, they require much more open space to hunt. They are designed for a fast, direct attack and are much less maneuverable than the similarly sized sharp-shinned hawk, which specializes in ambush, short blasts of speed, and highly maneuverable aerobatics to catch prey. But being predatory creatures capable of catching and killing a wide range of prey does not mean that kestrels have nothing to fear. To the contrary, they must be ever watchful that they do not fall victim to a larger predator. They occasionally fall prey to Cooper's hawks, peregrine falcons, owls, and even female sharp-shinned hawks.

In North America, kestrels were once called sparrow hawks. Homesick settlers exploring the New World frequently bestowed upon newly discovered animals the names of similar animals that they remembered from back home. The small, agile kestrels reminded them of the European sparrow hawks, which are, in fact, accipiters, not falcons.

American kestrels are falcons, every bit as much as peregrines, prairie falcons, or gyrfalcons. Physical traits shared by most falcons include the presence of a notched upper mandible, or tomial tooth, and long, pointed wings, with the first primary being noticeably shorter than the second and third, which are usually equal in length. The rounded tail is about two-thirds as long as the wings. Among American kestrels there is a great deal of variation in plumage, especially among males. Some individuals have a rust-colored spot on the top of the head, but in others it is barely noticeable. The amount of black barring and the richness in plumage coloration seem to be directly related to the birds' geographic location. The southernmost inhabitants—those in the Gulf Coast states—tend to be smaller and more richly colored than their northern and western counterparts.

The males are typically less heavily spotted than the females throughout the belly and flank regions. Among the first-year birds, or immatures, the males are usually much more heavily spotted than the females in the same nest, with some brownish streaking found throughout the breast and belly area, and the tail is tipped in brown, not white. The overall impression is that the plumage lacks the crispness in coloring and clarity of that of an adult bird. Young female kestrels are not as easily distinguishable from the adult females as are the males.

If you spend any time observing the plumage of an American kestrel, you can't help but notice those curious black spots on the back of the head and nape. Based on the size and placement of these spots it's easy to theorize their purpose. Called eye spots, these markings resemble the eyes and beak of the kestrel's face and could be a defense mechanism to thwart a possible attacker from approaching from behind. Many times a split second of hesitation on the part of the predator is all that is needed to alert the kestrel of impending danger and allow it to escape. Eye spots are also seen in many of the smaller owl species, such as the pygmy and elf owls.

Many field guides describe falcons as "round-headed" birds of prey. When a kestrel is sitting and relaxed, with its feathers puffed up, it can appear as though this is the case. Under most circumstances, however, the head is not round, but has a cube-like edginess, especially above the eye and down to the jaw area. The eyes, which upon first observation can appear black, are in fact a rich dark brown in color and are bright and alert.

The combination of its intense eyes with striking black vertical markings dividing bright white patches makes the American kestrel an unforgettable sight. It's easy to see why these beautiful little hunters have become such popular subjects for wildlife artists who express themselves in both two- and three-dimensional art. Over my many years of judging bird-carving shows, I've enjoyed seeing the many creative ways in which American kestrels have been portrayed. In this context, kestrels far outnumber other species of raptors—and for good reason. With their small songbird size and multicolored plumage, they are very appealing. And the fact that they are predators provides a wide range of compositional possibilities. The kestrel is an enchanting subject worthy of its prominent status among bird carvers and painters.

Top: This male perched atop a cable exhibits a beautiful and well-balanced pose.

Middle: Suspended aloft, a graceful American kestrel scans the ground below, ever watchful for any slight movement that may reveal its next meal.

Bottom: A pair of first-year males perch atop the branches of a tree during fall migration.

5

A mated pair of kestrels near their nest box. The female has a vole in her left foot.

RON AUSTING

A female kestrel approaching the nest hole with a vole. This photo illustrates a beautiful flight position of the wings and feet.

RON AUSTING

A female kestrel in the nest box feeding her hungry brood. Typically, the firstborn is the largest and strongest of the nestlings and is fed first.

RON AUSTING

Left: A brood of female kestrels just prior to attaining their adult plumage and about a week away from their first flight.

Bottom left: A rare look at an albino female kestrel clearly shows the contouring of the chest, breast, and belly feathers.

Bottom right: This clear photo of the underside of a kestrel male's tail shows the unique patterning.

RON AUSTING

RON AUSTING

7

An extreme close-up of the feet reveals a reptilian scale pattern common among birds of prey. Note the dynamic angle of the outer toe. Details such as this do much to enhance the carving.

Another photo of feet, in a different position, shows the extreme flexibility inherent in the toes. Notice the webbing that is found connecting the middle and outside toes. This is an important detail often overlooked.

A nice close-up portrait of an adult female shows the relationship between the eyes and the beak. Feather flow off the breast and onto the upper wing is evident as well.

RON AUSTING

Top left: As the head rotates, little or no deflection occurs on the upper chest region.

Top right: When viewed from behind, the female kestrel shows the same distinctive head spots found on the male.

Left: An extremely rare photo of a pair of American kestrels sharing a fence with their close cousin, a merlin. Outwardly, it is easy to see that these two distinct species are closely related. This image was captured by the great Ron Austing during fall migration in Cape May, New Jersey.

Curiosity comes to mind when viewing this picture of an adult male. Especially endearing are the puffy feathers that stick out from the throat region beneath the beak.

A close-up profile of the head of an adult male clearly shows the black markings that make the kestrel so easily identifiable.

Feather flow can be clearly seen in this close-up head picture of an adult male. Note the clearly delineated line of light feathers separating the head and the chest, and the sharp blue lines flowing through the forehead region.

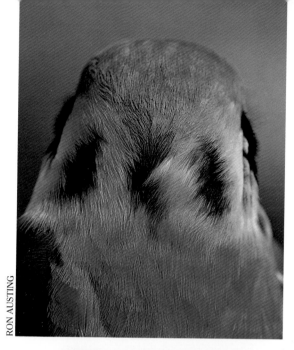

Top left: Attention must be given to feather flow as it cascades toward the back of the head. A visual traffic jam of color and texture occurs in this region.

Top right: An interesting three-quarter back view of the head of a male kestrel shows the feather flow as it radiates out from the front of the eye region onto the beak and cere.

Left: A close-up of the folded primaries and top of tail reveals the light edging, which must be carefully rendered to ensure accuracy.

Top left: Dynamic areas such as these side pocket feathers cry out for super detailing and accurate brush control to amplify feather flow and softness.

Top right: This picture focuses on the scapular and nape regions and how they relate to the overall position of the back feathering. No deflection occurs, even when the head is in an extreme turn.

Left: This photo of a typical clutch of American kestrel eggs reveals their round shape and brown spots. Rarely are more than five eggs laid at a time.

RON AUSTING

Top left: Front view of an adult female showing the area at which the legs connect to the body. This is a very soft, furlike area best rendered by texturing with a stone rather than a burner.

Top right: A full-body profile of an adult female, showing good balance and streamlined shape. Notice that the tips of the primary feathers fall far short of the end of the tail.

Left: The same pose with a slightly different head angle shows the extreme flexibility inherent in the neck vertebrae.

Top left: This three-quarter back view of the whole body of a resting adult male shows a pleasing layout and the relationships of the various feather groups. This pose would translate into a beautiful carving.

Top right: Front view of an adult male showing a relaxed yet semialert pose. The legs are mostly covered by belly feathering. Notice the size, shape, and position of the black markings found on the outer portion of the belly region. Details like this are very important and must be rendered accurately.

Left: A full back view of a standing male kestrel shows the various black bars and markings found on the body, starting at the tail and ending up at the back of the head.

CHAPTER TWO

Getting Started

BAND SAW BASICS FOR BIRD CARVERS

Owning quality woodworking machinery and knowing how to set it up and operate it safely can be a real timesaving advantage. If you are planning on doing any type of three-dimensional carving, you will eventually want to purchase a band saw. Removal of excess material from a thick block of wood accurately and efficiently will enable you to begin the process of carving and shaping the bird with a great deal more confidence.

When considering buying a band saw, do your homework. Talk to other experienced woodworkers and carvers. Above all, avoid bargains and don't skimp on quality. (A list of quality manufacturers can be found in the Appendix.) A good-quality, well-maintained band saw is one of the most important woodworking machines in any wood shop. No other tool allows you to cut curves and an infinite variety of shapes in thick wood with the ease and speed of a band saw.

I have a 20-inch vertical Powermatic model 81 band saw with a $12^{1}/_{2}$-inch depth of cut. This is a big, heavy, powerful machine that, in addition to bird carving, I often use for applications such as resawing boards, slicing veneer stock, and even cutting intricate dovetail joints. I also have a 14-inch Delta band saw with a 6-inch riser block set up in my studio for smaller work.

Choosing the correct blade for your particular type of cutting is very important for achieving optimum results. A band saw blade is a thin, flexible ribbon of steel with sharp teeth milled onto one edge. I cannot overstate the importance of using the highest-quality blades possible and maintaining the correct blade tension. Blade selection is dictated by the thickness of the wood being cut, its hardness, and the tightness of the curves that will need to be cut.

Today's blades are highly refined and complex. Modern band saw blades are available in widths ranging from $^{1}/_{8}$ inch up to and exceeding $1^{1}/_{4}$ inches. The wider the blade is, the thicker the steel that makes up the blade. Band saw blades are available

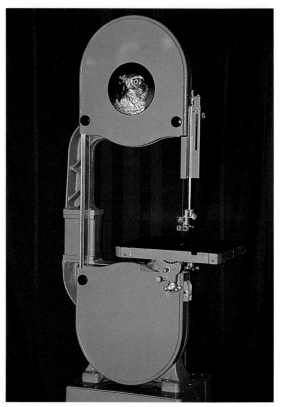

My "heavy artillery" band saw is one of my favorite tools. Pictured is a 1964 Powermatic model 81 20-inch vertical band saw. This machine is indispensable for cutting out larger birds and resawing rough-cut lumber. Note the dust collector hose, which is hooked up to an industrial dust collection system. This allows for virtually dust-free sawing. This saw is capable of accepting blades from 1/8-inch to 3/4-inch cutting capacity.

My 14-inch 1975 Rockwell model 28 band saw has been modified with the addition of a 6-inch riser block. Custom additions like these are available from the manufacturer or can be ordered through any reputable woodworking tool dealer. This block increases the cutting depth from 6 inches to 12 inches.

in four different types of tooth forms: hook, skip, regular, and variable. The efficiency at which a band saw blade will cut through a particular type of wood, regardless of its thickness, is directly affected by the blade's tooth form. For example, when cutting through a 10-inch-thick block of tupelo with a regular fine-tooth blade, the gaps between the teeth will load up prior to exiting the stock and increase friction, thus slowing down your cut and possibly overheating and damaging the teeth.

In my shop I always have an assortment of blades available for different situations. I have found that a 1/4-inch-wide hook-tooth blade is ideally suited for cutting out songbird-size to

This is what the shop looks like after a typical day of band saw work. All of these scraps pictured will ultimately become songbirds or important parts of future carvings. Knowing that good tupelo is hard to come by, I try to waste as little of it as possible.

much larger birds in various thicknesses of either tupelo or basswood. The hook-tooth blade is simply a more highly refined and aggressive form of the outdated skip-tooth design and is the best choice when cutting through thick, medium-density woods.

When operating a band saw, remember the following to ensure a lifetime of safe cutting:

- Wear eye protection.
- Avoid alcoholic drinks prior to and during usage.
- Use some type of dust collection system hooked up to your band saw.

Basswood and tupelo are the two most commonly used woods in decorative bird carving today. Subtle differences exist between the two, and it is a matter of personal preference as to which would work best for you. Basswood is denser and can be grainier.

- Keep hands on both sides and away from the moving blade.
- Always keep your eyes on the cutting area.
- Keep your immediate work area clean.
- Keep the blade guide no more than 1/4 inch above the top of the block being cut.
- Maintain proper blade tension.
- Don't force the work into the cutting blade.
- Pay attention to your work and avoid distractions.

CHOOSING YOUR WOOD

The two species of wood most commonly used by the vast majority of bird carvers working today are tupelo (*Nyssa* spp.) and basswood (*Tilia americana*). (Suppliers are listed in the Appendix.) Both woods have properties that make them ideally suited for decorative bird carving—they are lightweight, resistant to checking or cracking, and easily workable. The most important difference between the woods is found in their intended use. Carvers who prefer edge tool carving, using knives and chisels, tend to prefer basswood because of its grain structure and clean finish once a cut is made. Basswood, or linden, is a favorite among caricature and relief carvers.

Decorative bird carvers as a general rule tend to be a bit more mechanized in their approach to carving and rely on power equipment to remove wood. Tupelo lacks the grain structure found in basswood and therefore is more workable and won't fuzz up when high-speed abrasive stones are used to create surface contours and when sculpting feathers. Cross-grain ridging is generally not as pronounced with tupelo, although I've wrestled with some very grainy tupelo at times.

Knots are rare in both woods when milled correctly. Both woods can be sanded easily, yielding a satiny smooth surface perfect for texturing. Basswood, due to its denser property, can be burned tighter with a closer, cleaner burn than tupelo, which is softer, although more effort is needed to remove any traces of surface fuzz prior to burning. You may want to try both woods to determine which one works best for you.

DRAWING YOUR OWN PATTERNS

As a beginning bird carver's ability to carve develops and improves, one of the most difficult transitions to make is to stop relying on someone else's patterns. Knowing how to transform an idea or mental image into a workable pattern gives you the freedom to create original and unique works of art.

By following a few simple steps and using three basic shapes, you can create patterns for any bird you wish to carve. Begin with the side view. Coincidentally, it all starts with an egg. This simple shape forms the body of the bird. It can be elongated for slimmer birds or rounded for puffy, shorter-profiled birds.

Once you've established the body shape, add a rectangle to the top of the wider part of the egg shape. The size of this rectangle is determined by the head shape, including the bill length, of the bird you are going to carve. Leave a little extra material in the head and neck region to allow for the slight modifications that always seem to occur during the carving process, such as turning the head to one side or having the bird looking up.

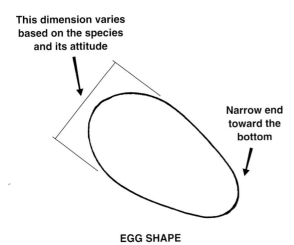

This dimension varies based on the species and its attitude

Narrow end toward the bottom

EGG SHAPE

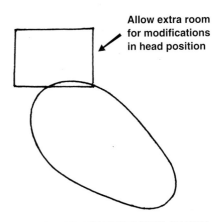

Allow extra room for modifications in head position

EGG SHAPE AND RECTANGULAR BOX

19

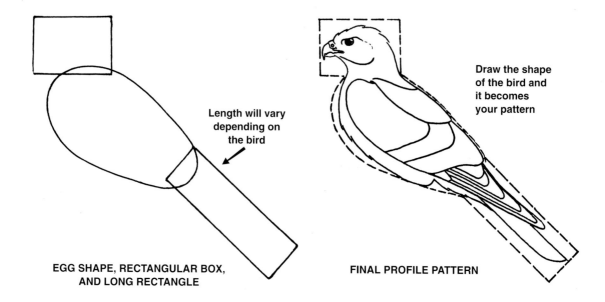

**EGG SHAPE, RECTANGULAR BOX,
AND LONG RECTANGLE**

Length will vary
depending on
the bird

Draw the shape
of the bird and
it becomes
your pattern

FINAL PROFILE PATTERN

Now add a longer, narrower rectangle to the lower portion of the egg shape. The length of this rectangle is directly related to the tail length of your subject. The angle of this shape can be varied considerably, depending on the attitude of the bird. Drawing the top view of your bird is much easier, because you already have the sizes and shapes of your three basic parts. The only modification you may wish to make is to open up the tail. To do this, simply redraw the long rectangle into a fan shape, maintaining the same length at the center.

The ability to draw accurately takes lots of practice. The more you do it, the better you will become. Be an observer, and train yourself to notice details. That pathway from your eyes to your drawing hand needs a lot of use in order to smooth out the bumps. I recommend that you purchase a pad of inexpensive drawing paper, and practice pencil control by smoothly drawing basic geometric and rounded shapes. With patience and repetition, you will improve.

Once you have drawn the top and side views of your bird, place carbon paper between the drawings and a flexible piece of clean, heavy paper or cardboard, and transfer the shape of your bird onto it. Using a sharp knife or a good pair of scissors, cut out your patterns. You are now ready to proceed to the block of wood.

When drawing your patterns onto the wood, I recommend allowing an inch or two on both ends of the block to allow for grain abnormalities such as cracks, checks, or embedded stones. Draw the profile first. Now you are ready to begin removing wood.

CHAPTER THREE

Design and Composition

Regardless of how well one can carve and paint a bird, proper design and composition—the considered arrangement of the various parts of a work of art and how they relate to one another—are a very important component of the final product.

I've always admired certain artists who have a knack for putting all the elements in the right places to create vibrant sculptures. Just how does one know or learn how to do this? Most of the artists I know would have a hard time explaining this, as they rely on their instincts and work intuitively. Others take a more methodical route and carefully plan out every detail in advance, leaving nothing to chance. Whichever route is taken, no decision is arbitrary. Every ingredient, from the size and shape of the branch or support structure to the color of the base, affects the overall outcome.

To ensure maximum impact, the bird should be well placed as the central focus of the work. A well-balanced composition creates a better feeling in the viewer than a busy, chaotic tangle. However, a composition that is too symmetrical can appear artificial and be boring and static. A composition is successful if every element falls into place and acts to complement the main subject, the bird. Think of everything but the bird as being the frame around a painting—there to enhance, not compete.

Most displays are based, either knowingly or unknowingly, on a rectangle, which is one of the most versatile and workable shapes. The rectangle can either stand vertically or lie on its side. Since their bases are flat, rectangles, squares, and triangles appear much more anchored and stable than arcs and circular shapes. The curved nature of a circular arrangement gives the impression of freedom and movement. A flowing line gives the eye little time to rest, so compositions governed by circles and flowing arcs would work best when you wish to animate your bird, as in a flight pose.

A very powerful element of design for creating dramatic action is the diagonal line. A well-balanced composition with

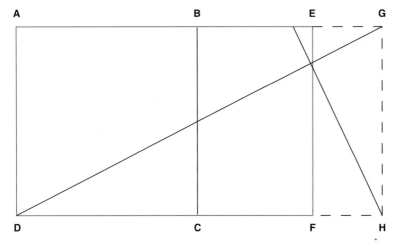

A   B   E   G

D   C   F   H

strong diagonal thrust will lead the eye rapidly across the piece, creating the illusion of space and depth and suggesting movement.

Some rectangular shapes appear more pleasing and balanced to the eye than others. The ancient Greeks based the design and layout of their ancient temples and sculptures on a set of proportions that they felt reflected the harmony of the universe. Artists and architects of the Renaissance period used this ratio and relied on it so much that it was pronounced "divine" and referred to as the golden ratio. To do this, draw two adjoining squares, ABCD and BGHC. Then draw a diagonal line connecting D to G and intersect this line at a right angle from H. Draw a vertical line EF, and the result will be a golden rectangle, AEFD.

When your goal is to create a visually pleasing sculpture with the bird as the main subject, your objective is to tell a story, rather than just make bird statues. You want to convey to the viewer as much information about the bird as possible.

Learning to portray moods can be very effective. Pay attention to your own moods, such as relaxation, nervousness, aggression, fear, passivity. Your body dynamic speaks volumes about your state of emotion. Similarly, the outward physical appearance of a bird reflects its health, state of being, and intent. For instance, when a bird is relaxed and settled on its perch, it has the appearance of calmness and stability. The body feathers are looser and may appear a bit puffy, and the eyelids take on an elliptical shape. It would appear strange indeed to try to portray your bird as relaxed, yet have the feathers tightly compacted and the head extended a bit with saucerlike round eyelids, as if it were ready to take flight. Subtlety in the bird's pose and an understanding of avian anatomy will yield much more accuracy in your final product. Spend time watching birds as they interact with their environments, and you will learn a lot.

When you are planning your piece, consider the following: What is the bird doing? Is it resting or active? Has it just caught prey or is it in pursuit of prey? For a resting bird, the composition should convey stability, with a square, rectangular, or triangular shape. For an active bird, use circular and/or diagonal elements, such as circles, arcs, or sloping lines. To show pursuit or flight, use a strong diagonal or circular presentation. You may wish to combine some of these elements. The only limiting factor is your own creativity and artistic vision.

CHAPTER FOUR

Cutting the Profiles

It makes good sense to have a predetermined strategy in place before you make the first cut. Choose a nice, dry piece of either tupelo or basswood, and be sure it is free of knots, splits, and any odd discolorations that may indicate a hidden problem. Over the years, I've uncovered bullets, rocks, nails, and other surprises. Choose a block of wood that is slightly larger than the pattern; the extra wood allows for any eventualities such as fine splitting on the end grain or changes in head direction or shape.

Choosing the right piece of wood comes from experience. Its weight, color, and grain prominence all factor into its usability; avoid heavy or imbalanced pieces. The color should be a consistent light cream and the end grain should be free of splits and checks. It helps to run the block through a jointer prior to laying down the pattern to provide a smooth surface.

A band saw is used to trim the edges off the block. This can be a real time-saver, but be careful. The band saw will have a tendency to grab the wood and force it out of your hands. Use extreme caution. It only takes a split second of carelessness for an accident to happen.

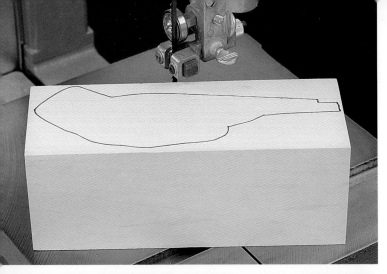

The profile is drawn onto a block of tupelo. The blade guide of the band saw is set 1/4 inch above the top of the block to ensure accuracy.

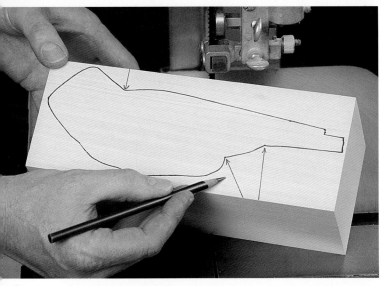

Clearance cuts are made at vital points on the block. These are cut first. This prevents the blade from binding.

Once the clearance cuts have been made, band sawing begins. I prefer to cut the top and longest sections first.

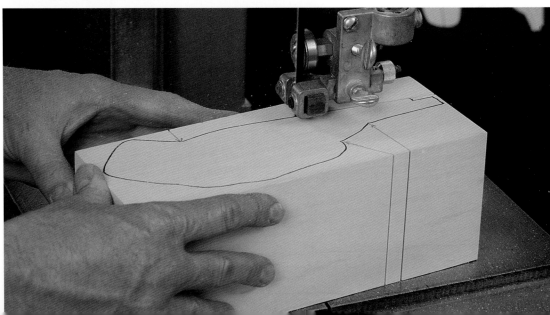

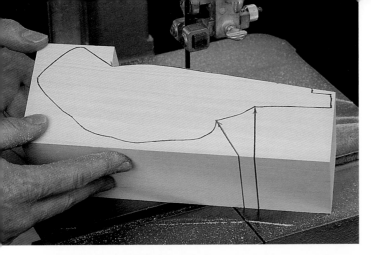

The resulting first cut. Try to stay to the outside of the line to prevent going off track and removing too much wood.

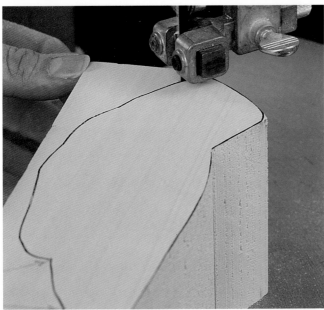

It's very important to maintain control of the block at all times. Be aware of the location of your fingers in relation to the moving blade. It only takes a second of carelessness to lose a finger.

The band saw is an invaluable machine for cutting curves in thick wood.

The final and shortest of the cuts occurs near the tail section.

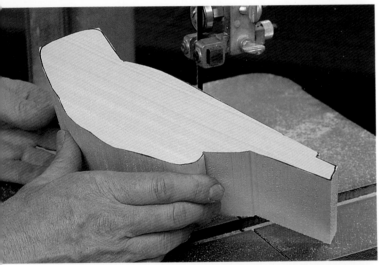

The completed profile.

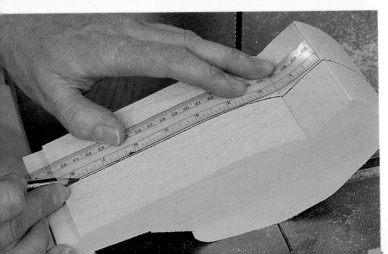

A flexible ruler comes in handy when laying out the centerline onto the block.

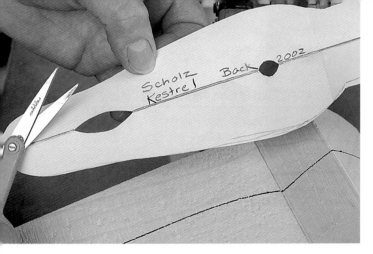

The back pattern has "windows" cut along the centerline for ease in aligning the pattern with the centerline on the block of wood.

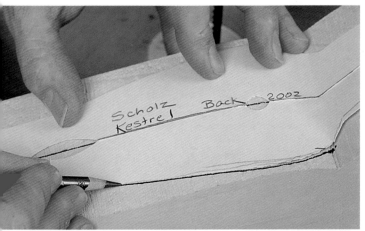

Press firmly onto the pattern while tracing it to prevent slipping.

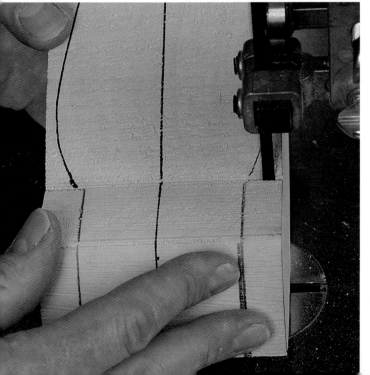

Two stop cuts are made up near the shoulder region first.

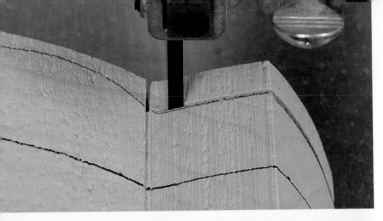

Excess wood is now removed from the head block region.

Hold on very tightly when band sawing an uneven and unstable form, as the saw has a tendency to grab the wood.

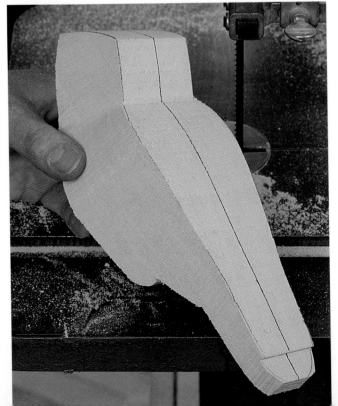

The profile and top have now been cut.

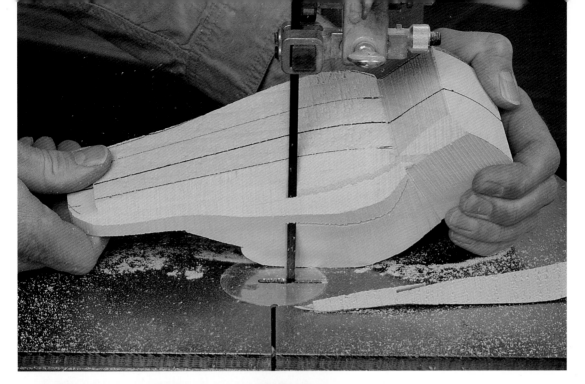

Top: I highly recommend that you have some experience using a band saw prior to trimming your block in this manner. It's a highly efficient way of removing wood, yet it can be very dangerous if you don't pay attention. I call this "peeling the potato."

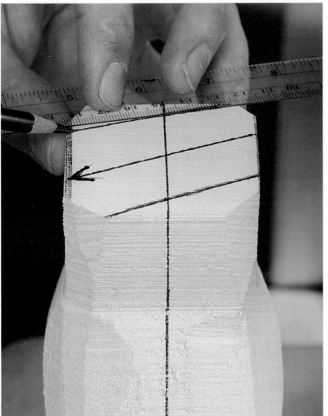

Left: The head width is now established, and the resulting waste wood will be removed from either side. The arrow indicates the direction that the bird will be looking.

I always leave a little extra wood when doing this, as experience has taught me that inevitably subtle changes will be made.

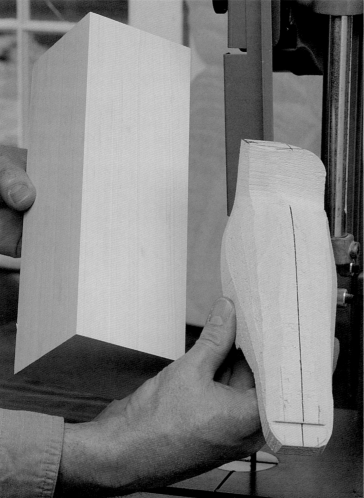

About fifteen minutes of careful band saw work can save a great deal of time when roughing out the body block. Note the direction of the grain.

CHAPTER FIVE

Blocking in the Body and Head

Once the bird has been band sawed to shape, you will begin establishing form and symmetry to the body. If you carved away the back centerline, redraw it immediately, beginning with the upper part of the body just below the head, and working your way downward toward the tail area. The objective is to form a well-balanced and proportional mass.

A soft lead pencil is useful for drawing onto the block. At this point, spend a lot of time studying the subject, as this is the most critical stage in the carving process. I call this establishing the foundation. No matter how well you can carve and texture feathers, if the body is not in balance and symmetrical, it will not look good regardless of what you do. A Foredom flexible-shaft tool works very well for this operation, using a 1-by-1-inch rubber sanding drum covered with a 1-by-2-inch sanding sleeve. It's best to use 80-grit to 100-grit, as it doesn't cut too quickly and leaves a smooth surface on which to draw. You are not dictated by grain direction the way you would be if you were using a knife or chisel.

Once the body has been shaped, you can begin work on the head block. Accurate patterns aid in proper wood removal. When reducing wood around the head region, proceed slowly so as not to remove too much wood. The tolerances in this area are much tighter, so pay attention. Once the head block is rough-shaped, sand it smooth so the patterns and, most importantly, the centerline can be accurately drawn in place. Maintain the centerline, as you will refer back to it many times.

The combination of replaceable sanding drums and the Foredom 44T handpiece is highly efficient for shaping and sanding the bird during the roughing-out process. The benefits of this method are that you are not dictated by grain direction, and the resulting surface is smooth and ready to be drawn onto.

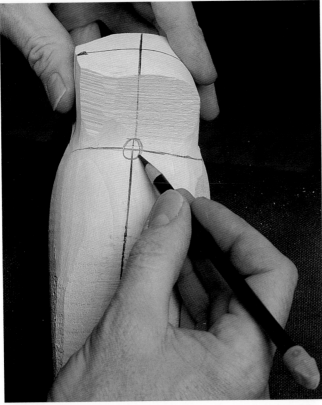

This intersecting point provides the spot where many of the critical measurements will originate. It approximates where the neck vertebrae join the backbone.

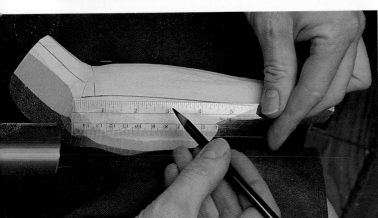

It's helpful to draw a horizontal line bisecting the sides to use as a reference when shaping the body. This aids in maintaining symmetry and balance.

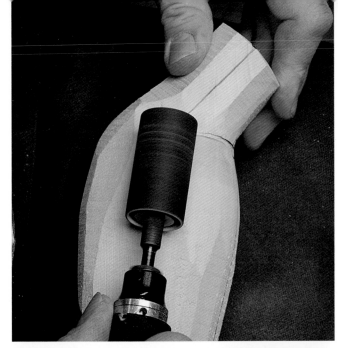

The initial cut is made starting at the back and rounding the scapular and wing area.

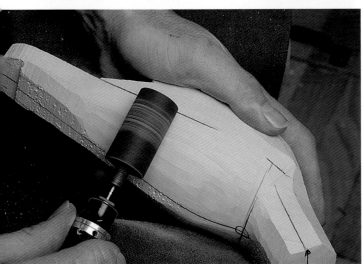

Once the rounding over is completed, long, consistent cuts are made from the upper wing region to the end of the tail. It is important to maintain consistency and avoid choppy strokes when doing this.

The other side is shaped to match the first series of cuts.

Your objective is a symmetrical area.

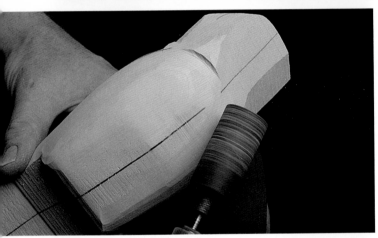

Follow the same procedure when rounding the chest, breast, and belly areas.

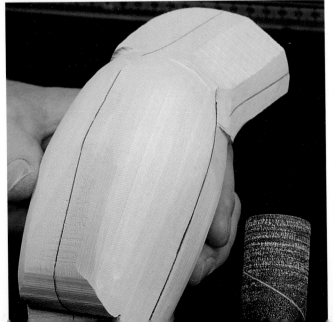

General shaping is now completed.

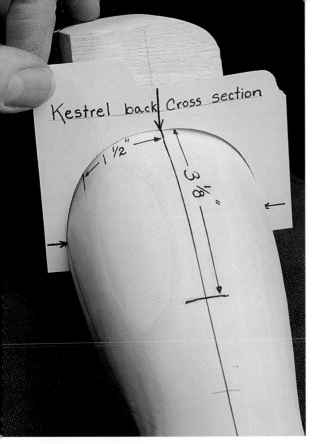

Kestrel back Cross section

1 ½"

3 ⅛"

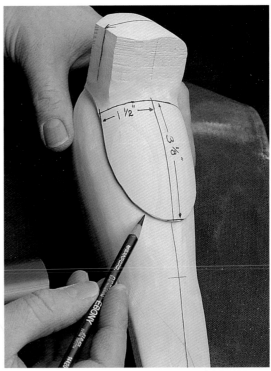

1 ½"

3 ⅛"

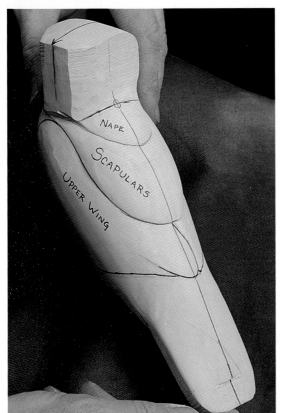

NAPE

SCAPULARS

UPPER WING

Top left: It is very helpful to use a paper template to ensure accuracy and balance.

Top right: The scapular region is the first major feather group to be blocked in. Rely on accurate measurements, and don't deviate from them.

Left: The rudimentary shapes and positions of the various wing components are now drawn in. Be careful to maintain the centerlines at all times.

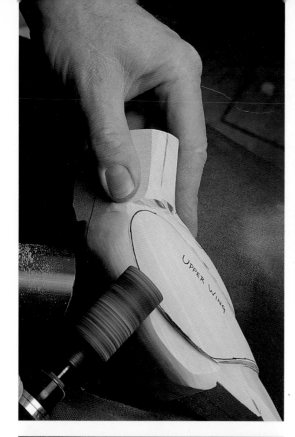

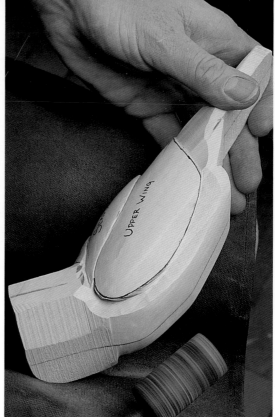

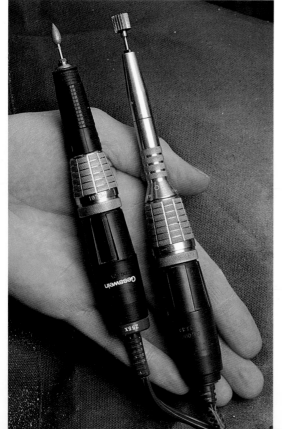

Top left: The wood below the leading edge of the left wing is being removed. The depth of cut averages around 1/4 inch.

Top right: The upper wing has now been isolated, and the chest and belly area can now be rounded over to near its final dimension.

Left: Once the roughing-out procedure is completed, it's time to begin refining your choice of tools. This combination of a standard handpiece and a slender head attachment to the Gesswein tool seems to work really well. The two cutters pictured are a 3/8-inch serrated stump cutter and a #3 medium-grit ruby flame cutter.

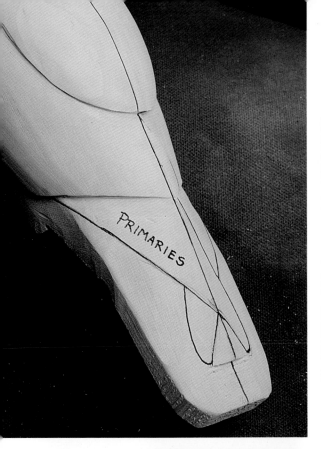

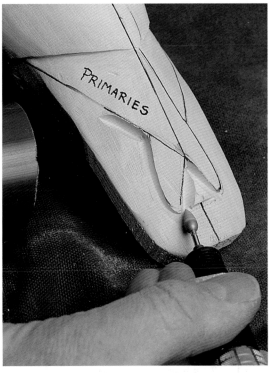

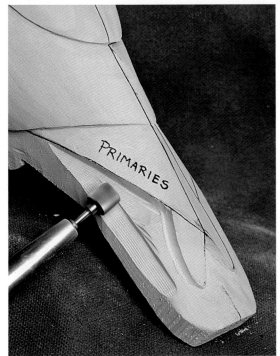

Top left: It is now time to isolate the primary feathers and shape the top of the tail. Careful layout of these rather complex feather groups is essential.

Top right: The #3 ruby flame cutter seems to work best for accurately outlining the wingtips. Depth of cut is approximately 1/8 inch.

Left: After outlining the primaries, a stump cutter is used to establish the top surface of the tail. Make your cuts really straight and clean, as these are long, stiff feathers.

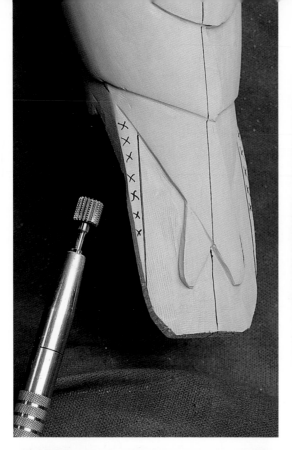

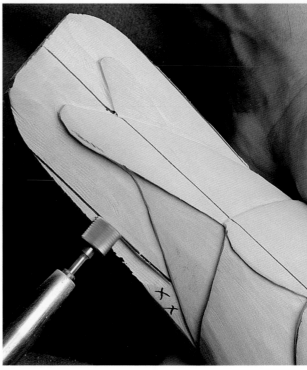

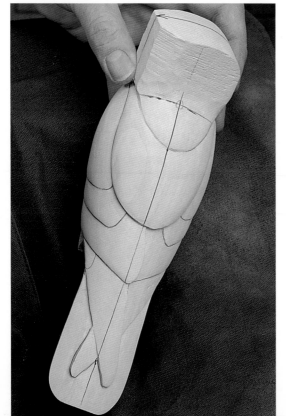

Top left: At this point, the final width of the tail is laid out, and the excess wood marked by X's is removed from either side. The overall width of the tail is 2 inches.

Top right: The stump cutter mounted in the slender head works well for this operation.

Left: The shaped and sanded back section, with all the major feather groups accurately laid out, is now ready for the feathers to be drawn in. A smoothly sanded surface helps when you draw the feathers.

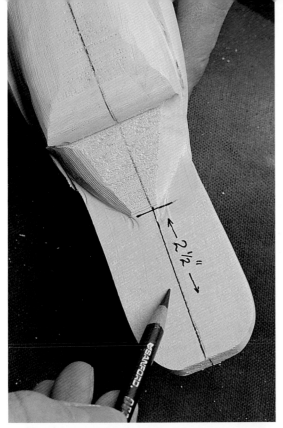

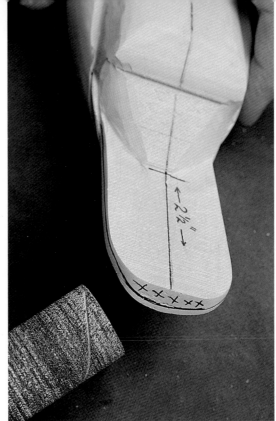

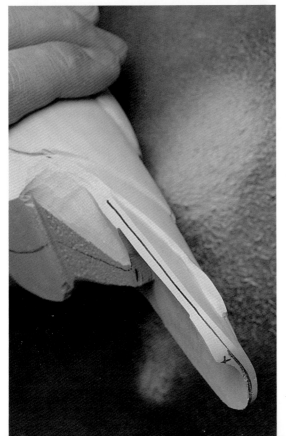

Top left: The undertail coverts will be formed as a result of the concave shape of the underside of the tail.

Top right: The drum sander mounted on the Foredom makes quick work of wood removal in this area.

Left: It is absolutely critical to maintain a parallel surface while shaping the tail down to near its final thickness. The thickness at this point is 1/8 inch.

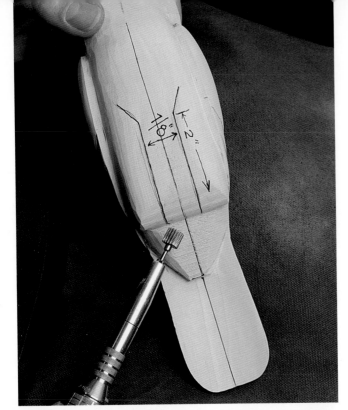

Removal of the area between the legs is now accomplished using the stump cutter and slender head combination. Leave lots of extra wood for the tarsus area from which the legs will protrude.

This area is nearing its final shape and dimensions.

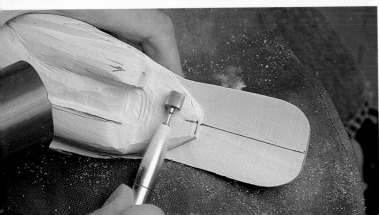

It is now time to do the final shaping of the undertail covert feathers. This area is composed of soft, billowy, hairlike feathers, so make it appear puffy.

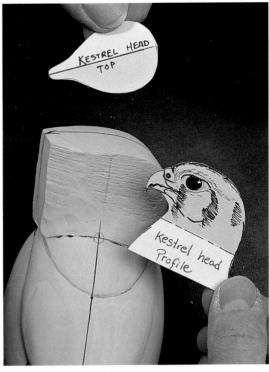

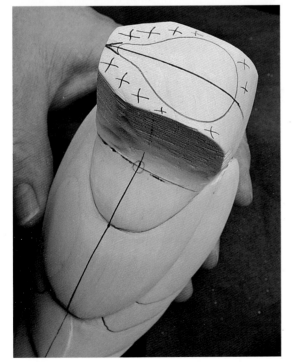

Top left: The completed underside, now ready for contouring and, ultimately, feathering.

Top right: Accurate patterns are a must when shaping the head block. Shown are a profile pattern and a top pattern.

Left: The top pattern is drawn in first, and the excess wood is carefully removed. The left side of the head block forms a bell shape as it resolves into the nape area.

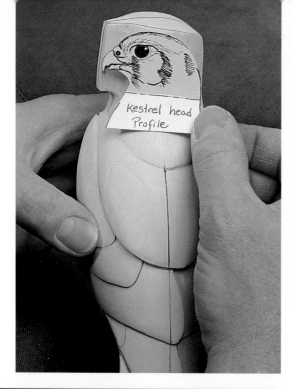

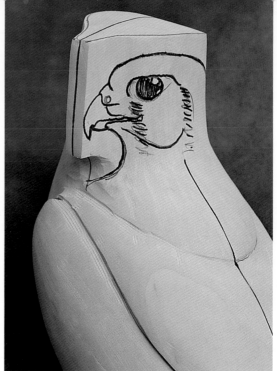

Top left: Once the width of the head has been established, the profile pattern is traced onto the head block. It's at this stage that you can incorporate mood and feeling into the bird's posture. By allowing extra wood, you have the flexibility to angle the pattern upward or downward. Note how the lower portion of the pattern is bent upward to allow for easy handling. Subtleties like this make a big difference.

Top right: The profile has been traced and is now ready to be shaped. The stump cutter and slender head combination works best for this.

Left: The kestrel is now beginning to take shape. All of the major flight feathers have been drawn in and are now ready to be carved.

CHAPTER SIX

Contouring and the Feathering Process

To really understand the nature of a bird's feathers, you must take several factors into account. First and foremost, a bird in the wild is almost always exposed to the elements. They don't live in warm, dry, climatically controlled environments. They are outside twenty-four hours a day. Birds get rained on, wind-blown, and bombarded with ultraviolet rays from the sun. Add to this the fact that birds of prey like the kestrel must kill living animals to survive. Living animals that don't want to die will fight furiously to avoid being eaten. Taking into consideration the harsh environment in which birds live, you must avoid the temptation to make your carving look as though it just flew out of a beauty salon.

When drawing in the individual feathers, work to stagger the spacing between the feathers, and vary the depth when you are carving them in. We humans have a tendency to organize things into neat, uniform rows, and this can be one of the most difficult things to overcome when laying out the respective feather groupings. These birds are streamlined falcons, so lay out the feathers so that they have a clean, tapered flow and are not square or blocky.

American kestrels have twelve tail feathers, ten primary feathers, twelve to fourteen secondaries, three tertials, and twelve to fourteen secondary coverts. But it's not necessary to show each feather, as many of them get covered up when the tail and wings are folded. When feathering the scapulars, nape, and upper wings, don't be preoccupied with trying to get the numbers exact. I prefer to draw and carve in enough to give the overall effect of flow and feathering without making the area too busy and crowded. Once the flight feathers—tail, primaries, tertials, secondaries, and secondary coverts—are drawn in, begin carving with the tail and work your way up to the head. A Gesswein handpiece is my tool of choice, with either a fine stump cutter or a diamond cylinder run at high speed.

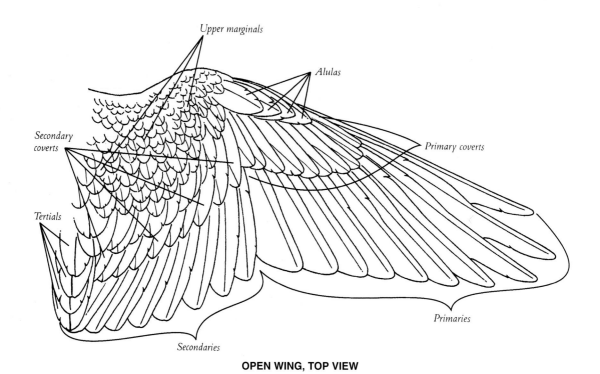

Upper marginals

Alulas

Secondary coverts

Primary coverts

Tertials

Primaries

Secondaries

OPEN WING, TOP VIEW

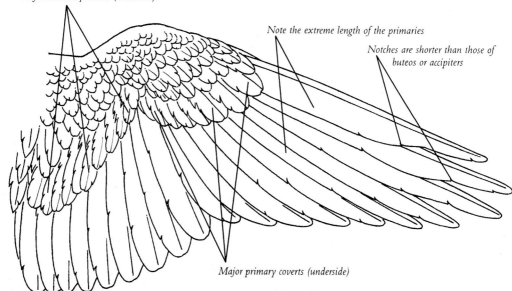

Major secondary coverts (underside)

Falcons' long, pointed wings facilitate high-speed flight at the expense of low-speed maneuverability

Note the extreme length of the primaries

Notches are shorter than those of buteos or accipiters

Major primary coverts (underside)

OPEN WING, BOTTOM VIEW

Full Back Layout Feather Map

Taking your carving experience to the next level by animating the bird can be a thrilling and rewarding experience. Birds are visually complex creatures and a good working knowledge of how their body parts fit together can be very helpful when creating a master carving. This full back layout is designed to help you understand the relationship and positioning of the spread tail and partially opened wings.

Note how the scapulars flare outward as the wings are extended. The alula feathers originate from up near the carpal, or wrist area, of each wing.

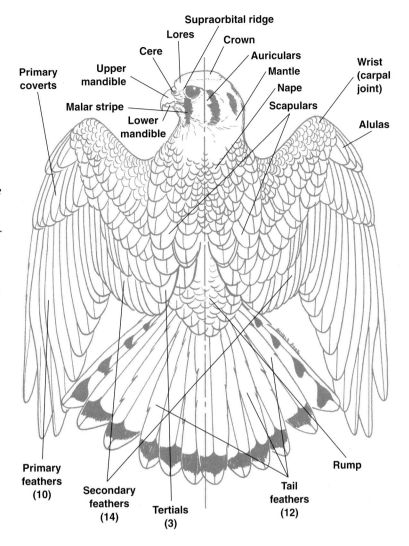

Supraorbital ridge
Lores
Cere
Crown
Auriculars
Mantle
Nape
Scapulars
Wrist (carpal joint)
Primary coverts
Upper mandible
Malar stripe
Lower mandible
Alulas
Primary feathers (10)
Secondary feathers (14)
Tertials (3)
Tail feathers (12)
Rump

The contouring, or "landscaping," of the rest of the body is accomplished with a 1/8-inch ruby ball carver run at high speed. The pencil line is outlined with the ruby ball, and all the excess wood is cut away below the feather, giving a scaly effect. Once this is completed, I prefer a slotted 1/8-inch mandrel with 220-grit sandpaper. A small orthodontal rubber band works nicely to hold it in place and can be rolled down along the shaft, easily allowing a change of sandpaper when the old piece wears out. My recommended sandpaper sequence is 150-grit, 320-grit, 600-grit, and then spray the entire bird with a light mist of isopropyl rubbing alcohol to raise the grain. Once dry, final sand with 600-grit wet or dry auto body paper (3M stock #411Q TRI-M-ITE).

Top left: A steady hand and accurate eye help when carving in these long, straight feathers. The cutter pictured is a fine serrated stump cutter.

Top right: Cleaning up and undercutting some of the feather groups can be done with a fine-pointed diamond cutter run at full speed.

Left: Layout and carving of the undertail feathers are best done after the top has been completed. It's easiest to shape these to their final thickness and avoid inaccuracies and possible breakage.

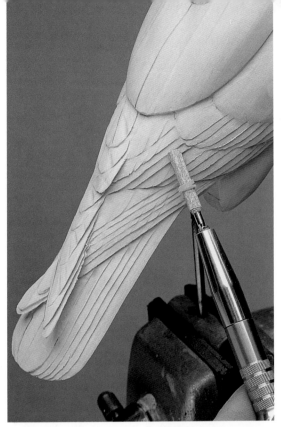

Left: A slotted mandrel is used along with 220-grit sandpaper to sand and put ripples into the feathers. A small rubber band holds the sandpaper in place. The tool is run at a slow speed to avoid burning and premature wearing out of the paper.

Bottom left: Directional arrows aid in the layout and in establishing directional flow during the contouring of the back region.

Bottom right: Grooves are cut into the wood surface with a #3 ruby flame and then subtly rounded over, creating the effect of hills and valleys. I refer to this as "landscaping" the surface.

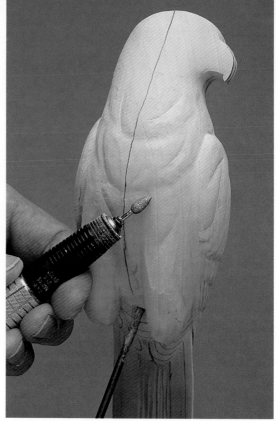

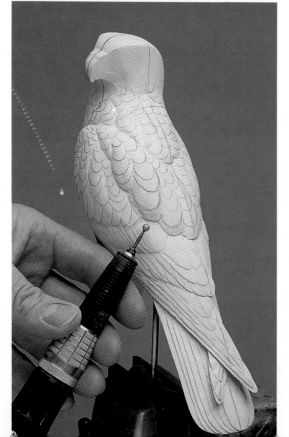

Top left: The same procedure is followed on the front. Notice that the arrows converge toward the centerline, amplifying the roundness and musculature of this area.

Top right: The #3 ruby flame is a valuable tool for this operation. The two arching areas isolate the pectoral muscles and crop region. I call these "necklaces."

Left: The contour feathers are drawn in all over the back region. They decrease in size as they near the head. A 1/8-inch ruby ball, run at high speed, is used to outline and carve away excess wood, forming all the humps and bumps.

Left: The area is outlined with the cutter bit and ready to have the lower portion of each feather carved away.

Bottom left: The area is ready for contour sanding. A slotted mandrel with 220-grit sandpaper is used to create a soft, subtle surface.

Bottom right: The area is now ready for final texturing.

Top left: At this stage, the sanding procedure is refined by using progressively finer sandpaper. My recommendation is to use 320-grit and finish with 600-grit.

Top right: A close-up of the completed primary and tail region, ready for feather shafts and burning texture.

Left: The underside areas are handled in the same way as the back. Always strive for subtlety and softness, and avoid any ledges and hard edges.

CHAPTER SEVEN

Carving and Shaping the Head

Once the top and profile of the head block have been rough-shaped, it's time to begin refining this very important region. The head and neck make up a small part of the falcon's overall anatomy, but I devote a disproportionately large amount of time to this area. You can texture under a microscope and have the painting ability of Rembrandt, but if you don't get the head, bill, and eye placement right, the bird will look unnatural. Take your time, and be absolutely certain of your measurements. It's helpful to look at a reverse image of the head in a mirror. This will give you a fresh look at your work, and you'll be surprised at how many imperfections become obvious. More than anything, the symmetry, or lack thereof, will be revealed. Draw in a crisp, straight centerline, and don't lose it.

The eye channels and lower mandible or jaw line are carved in using a 1/4-inch ruby ball (coarse grit) run at high speed (55,000 rpm). For both cuts, I've gone down about 3/16 inch. A common tendency for beginners is not to cut in deep enough, especially in the eye channels, which results in a bug-eyed look. When you think you've gone deep enough, go deeper!

Use a great deal of care when shaping the bill and cere area. A diamond cylinder works well to shape this area because it cuts smoothly and not too aggressively. The eyeholes are bored into the sides of the head at approximately a 40-degree angle to the top head centerline. Once the holes have been drilled, round over the edges with a fine, 3/16-inch diamond ball, and lightly sand the area with 220-grit paper.

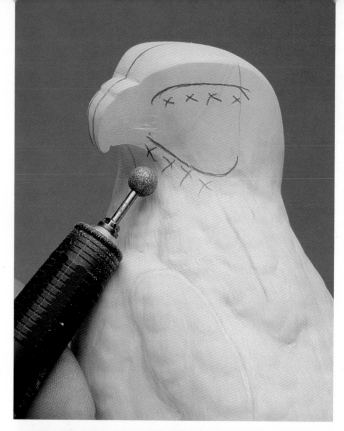

The two most critical cuts you will make are the eye channel and the jaw line. I use a 1/4-inch coarse-grit ruby ball run at high speed for this delicate bit of carving.

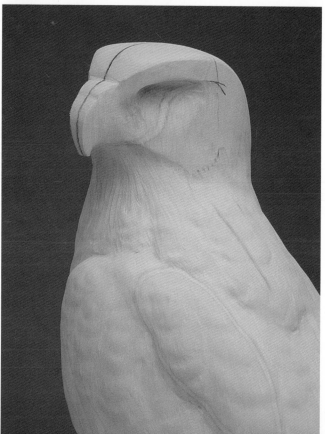

A common tendency is to not go deep enough when you remove wood for the eye channels. Many beginners are hesitant in this area, and their birds wind up with a bug-eyed look because the eyes are not being set deep enough.

Top left: The beak region is now carefully rounded over, and the shape becomes apparent.

Top right: The eye area is located, the cere has been sculpted into the beak, and the separation between upper and lower mandible has been drawn in.

Left: The entire head dynamic changes once the eyeholes have been drilled in. For this operation, I use a 1/4-inch wood bit. Remember: Measure twice before you cut to ensure accuracy. The outer rims of the eye sockets are rounded into the cavity. At this point, it's helpful to view your bird in a mirror, as this will reveal any irregularities in beak structure and eye placement.

CHAPTER EIGHT

Woodburning and Stoning for Texture

The importance of properly preparing the wood surface prior to texturing cannot be overstated. Extra care in the sanding process will greatly enhance the quality and efficiency of this critical last step in the carving process. It's not necessary to use sandpaper any finer than 600-grit for the final sanding of the bird's body. After the final sanding has been completed, I use a polished 1/8-inch burnishing ball to create subtle ripples in the feathers. This polishes the wood surface and gives the feathered area more volume. A Gesswein tool run at 55,000 rpm works great for this. Avoid making all the burnished lines the same length, and curve your strokes to create the illusion of roundness.

To replicate the texture of real feathers, you can use a specialized woodburning pen or, to create the illusion of the soft, fur-like feathering that is found in the undertail coverts, belly, and breast areas, a small, white cylinder mounted into a high-speed handpiece. The lines are then etched into the surface of the wood to create a soft directional flow. Whether to use a woodburner or the stoning process is a matter of personal technique and experience. When deciding which technique to use, consider three factors: the physical makeup of the area to be feathered; the final color of the area or bird; and whether you can see individual feathers within the overall grouping. Put simply, if the bird is white and you can't distinguish individual feathers on the body, as in a snowy egret or snowy owl, then it is a candidate for stoning texture. Birds such as golden eagles, most hawks and falcons, and game birds will benefit from being textured with a burning tool. Open yourself up to the creative possibilities that each technique offers. Remember, there is no one correct way. Use what works best for you and yields the best results on your carvings.

When burning in feather detail, a skew-shaped tip works best for the flight feathers, and a spade-shaped tip works best for the contour feathers. While burning my birds, I keep the heat setting quite low (not higher than a #3 setting on my Colewood Super

Pro). A common misconception is that a deeper burn will make your bird look softer. This is not true. It will take many more layers of paint to color the area, and a shiny buildup will occur.

The flight feathers are burned from the shafts to the outer edges of the feathers, whereas the contour feathers are burned from the outer edges inward. The gentle shading that results from these two techniques works to enhance the softness of the feathers once the paint has been applied. In the bird shown here, all of the back feathering and the top of the head have been textured with a burning pen. The throat area under the beak, breast, belly, legs, and undertail coverts have been textured with a white cylinder stone. Many carvers I know will stone texture first, and then enhance it by burning over the texturing.

Over many years of carving and teaching, I've found it best to delay the setting of the eyes until after most of the body texturing has been completed. The highly polished surface of a glass eye seems to be a magnet for a number of accidents, especially scratches. When you are ready to place the eyes permanently into the sockets, the surrounding area should be free of wood dust and sanded smooth to provide an even surface on which to blend the eyelid putty into the surrounding wood. The eyes are set into the sockets with two-part epoxy putty. The eraser end of a pencil works well to press and adjust the eyes to ensure proper focus and matching angles. The head is contoured and sanded smooth in preparation for final texturing. Once the eyelids are put in place and allowed to harden thoroughly overnight, the remaining areas around the eyes can be textured with a small, white 1/8-inch cylinder texturing stone.

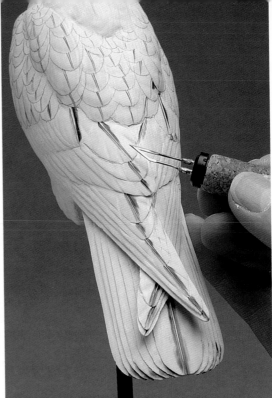

Top left: The final shapes and sizes of the contour feathers have been drawn on the surface of the finely sanded body. Feather shafts are located and staggered in a way that creates a rhythmic flow among the feathers. Feather shafts are also drawn onto the major flight feathers—tail, primaries, tertials, secondaries, and secondary coverts.

Top right: A long, pointed, skew-shaped burning tip is used to burn in the feather shafts, which are formed by the combination of heat and pressure on either side of each shaft. Keep the heat as low as possible to avoid scorching the wood surface.

Left: Sometimes I will go over the entire area with a polished burnishing ball. This, run at high speed, creates a highly polished, rippled surface on which to burn. This seems to add a bit more volume to the feathers. The burnishing strokes coincide with the direction of the feather barbs, which will be burned into the surface.

Top left: With a long, pointed skew tip and low heat, the burning has begun. My objective is a clean, tight, and most importantly, consistent surface.

Top right: The contour feathers of the upper wing are burned using a spade tip set at a fairly low temperature (#3 setting on a Colewood detailer). This burning technique differs from that used for the flight feathers in that the stroke is initiated from the outer edge of the feather and moves inward. This creates a subtle shading effect that will aid in an overall appearance of softness and flow.

Left: All of the major flight feathers and contour feathers of the upper wings, scapulars, and nape are now burned. This leaves the head, on which a great deal of attention will now be focused—not only in creating texture, but also in eye placement and lid detail.

Top left: The right side of the bird is completed and ready for paint. Special consideration will be given to the area directly behind the head, where three major feather tracks converge.

Top right: Over many years of carving and teaching, I've found it best to delay the setting of the eyes until after most of the body texturing has been completed. An 8mm, #120 glass eye on wire (available from Tohican Glass Eyes; see Appendix) is readied for insertion into the eye socket. Be sure to carve the eye socket deep enough that the eye will sit well inside of the brow.

Left: The eye is now set and adjusted in the socket using a two-part epoxy putty. Pictured is a homemade tool made of 1/8-inch copper wire flattened on one side and rounded at the tip. This configuration allows for accurate distribution and shaping of the eyelid and surrounding area.

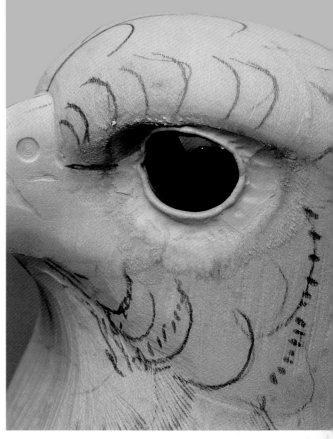

Top left: The preliminary eyelid is two-part epoxy putty rolled out into a 1/6-inch worm. It is then laid around the circumference of the eye in preparation for final shaping using the eye tool. Caution: The putty is water soluble, and using too much water will make it pasty and unworkable.

Top right: A close-up of the nearly completed eyelid shows the convergence in front of the eye directly on the pencil mark. This mark ensures balance and accuracy when viewed from the front. Excess putty is blended into the surrounding wood and will later be sanded smooth.

Left: Notice the difference in character and intensity between the finished and unfinished eyes.

Top left: The surrounding area of the head is now ready for contouring and, ultimately, texturing with the woodburner.

Top right: Focusing on the beak, the woodburner with a skew tip is used to delineate the upper and lower mandibles. Using the woodburner prevents the wood from splitting or breaking off at the fragile tip. If a knife blade were used, it would act like a wedge, possibly compromising this fragile area.

Left: The lower mandible is carved slightly narrower than the upper mandible. The edges are rounded inward, and the whole beak is sanded with 320-grit and then 600-grit sandpaper. Superglue is applied to the surface of the beak as an added strengthener. As it is absorbed into the wood surface, it hardens like plastic.

Top left: Directional flow lines are drawn in over the eye in preparation for contouring.

Top right: A ¹/₁₆-inch diamond ball run at high speed is used to carve in the humps and bumps throughout the head and neck region. Careful attention must be paid to areas directly surrounding the eye.

Left: A deeper groove is cut along the jaw line. This gives the region more definition.

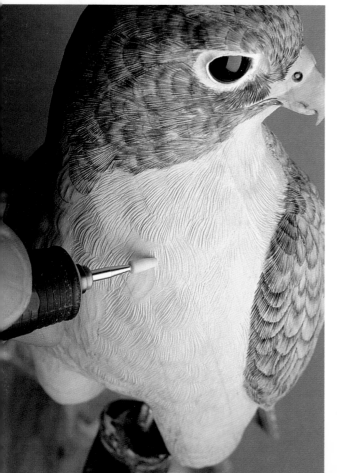

Top left: A slotted mandrel with 220-grit sandpaper is used to soften the edges of the contours.

Top right: The entire head has now been burned, and the nostrils are shaped. Very carefully, a white cylinder stone is used to texture the surrounding white putty close to the eye.

Left: The soft, furlike feathering found on the chest, breast, and belly area is stoned-in using a small, white cylinder run at high speed. It is very important to establish a definitive flow of the feathers to make this a vibrant and exciting area.

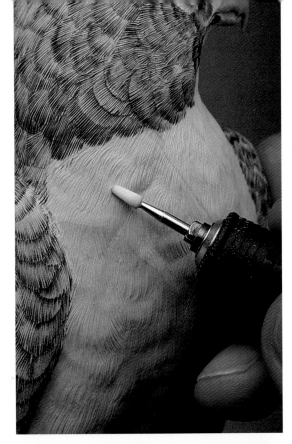

Top left: I occasionally go over certain areas to deepen splits and accentuate specific feather groups. This enlivens the flow.

Top right: As a final touch, the heat of the wood burner is increased, and areas where the dark malar stripes occur are accentuated. The kestrel is now ready for cleaning, then sealer.

Left: This is an excellent view of the completed stoned-in texture of the chest, breast, belly, and tarsus regions.

CHAPTER NINE

Legs and Feet

Creating realistic feet and legs is one of the most challenging and often overlooked areas of the entire bird-carving process. Often the feet appear as though they were quickly added as an afterthought, yet this is a highly expressive and extremely important element. Making the feet cannot be considered carving so much as construction, and every carver has his or her own methods. The feet can be made from metal, wood, or clay, depending on the size of the bird and whether they will be a supporting structure. For songbirds, I prefer copper wire and solder. To create the feet for the American kestrel, I carved the toes and talons individually from hard maple. The leg shafts are $1/8$-inch-thick brass rod cut to length and bent to the desired angles. Once the toes are carved and sanded, glue them to the leg shaft with five-minute epoxy. Two-part epoxy putty is used to build up the area where the toes join the legs. When this has hardened, a $1/8$-inch ruby ball works well to final shape the area. The talons have a drop of superglue applied for strength.

I strongly recommend experimenting with various materials and techniques to find which work best for you. Unless you are an expert with a soldering iron or a master welder, the standard process for making small bird feet can be intimidating. An easy alternative to the wire and weld method is to create the feet from clay, such as a two-part epoxy putty (available from Jaymes Company and many other well-stocked carving supply companies). This putty is quite strong when it has fully hardened and can be sanded and stoned to a variety of shapes. The trick is to work with the putty once it begins to firm up, as it will hold its shape and not be as sticky as when you first mix it. During the hardening process you'll have about an hour of work time before it gets too hard to shape. As with any endeavor, it will take some practice to achieve really good results.

Remember to keep an open mind and always experiment with new ideas and possibilities—we all have something to offer to this beautiful art form.

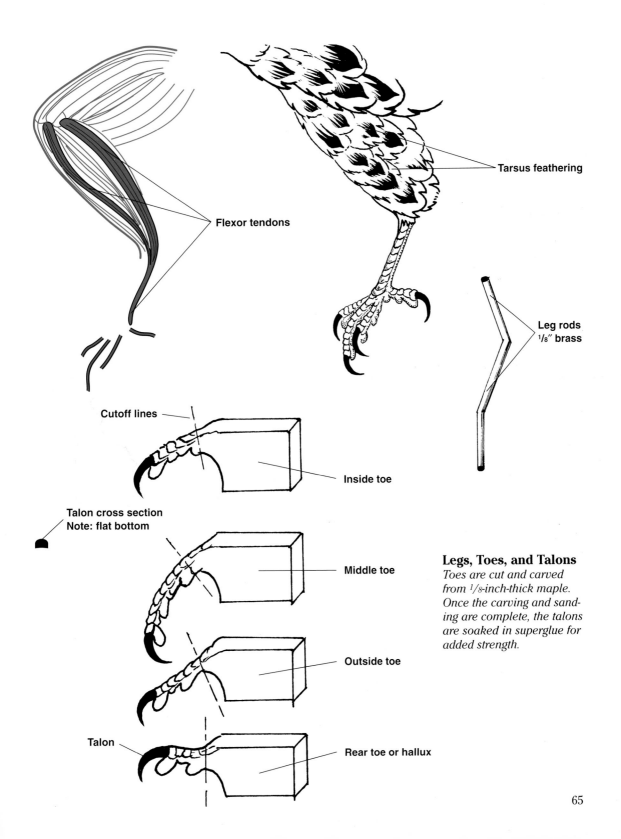

Flexor tendons

Tarsus feathering

Leg rods
1/8" brass

Cutoff lines

Inside toe

Talon cross section
Note: flat bottom

Middle toe

Outside toe

Talon

Rear toe or hallux

Legs, Toes, and Talons
Toes are cut and carved from 1/8-inch-thick maple. Once the carving and sanding are complete, the talons are soaked in superglue for added strength.

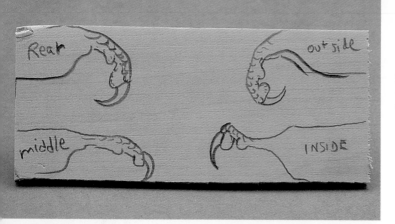

After careful study of American kestrel feet, draw the toes onto a piece of hardwood.

Oops! My ruler stretched when I measured the thickness of this piece of hardwood. It should read $1/8$-inch-thick hardwood, not $1/4$ inch as pictured. The toes are individually cut out of this stock and carved to shape. Once the toe is completed, superglue is applied to the talon for added strength. The tab at the end of the toe is useful to hold onto during the carving process. A fine jigsaw is useful for this delicate cutting operation.

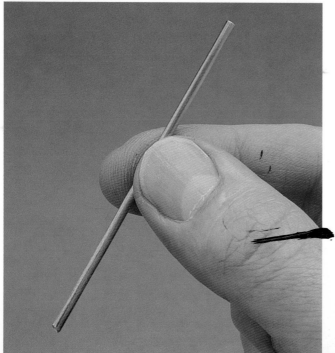

A $1/8$-inch brass rod forms the structural core of the American kestrel leg. These will be the only support of the bird, so strength and rigidity are important to consider. This unit is cut to 3 inches, and fine steel wool is used to polish and clean it.

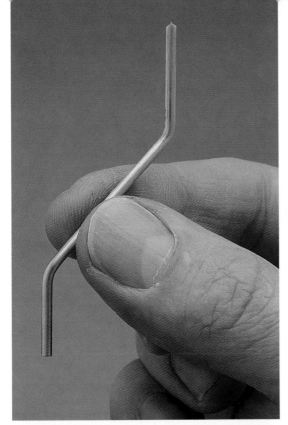

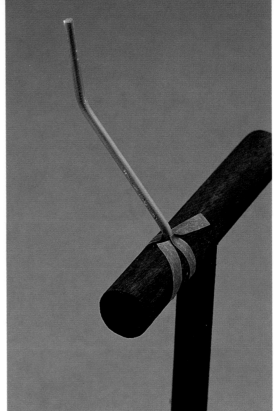

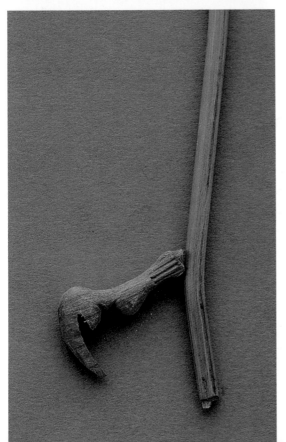

Top left: Measuring 3/4 inch in from each end, the ends are bent to the appropriate angles for the positioning and balance of the bird. Sometimes it is easier to do this first with a thinner, easier-to-bend wire, establishing the correct angles. This can then be used as a pattern, and the 1/8-inch brass can be bent using pliers to match it. The length of the leg from bend to bend is 1 1/2 inches.

Top right: A 1/8-inch hole is drilled vertically into the branch and the leg wire is inserted. At this point, thin strips of masking tape are used to lay out the angle and to position the four toes.

Left: This gives the idea of how attachment occurs. Once the toes are finished, they are epoxied onto a 1/8-inch brass rod and bent to the correct shape of the legs. It's helpful to have the bird up on the branch with the legs in place prior to gluing on the toes.

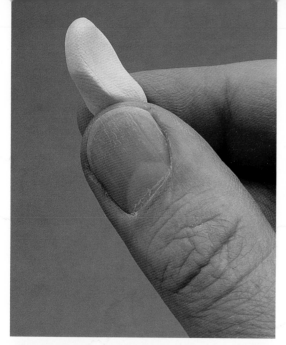

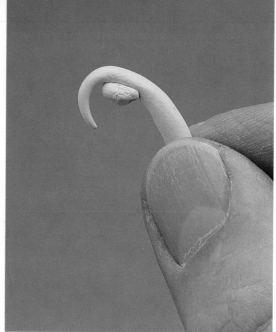

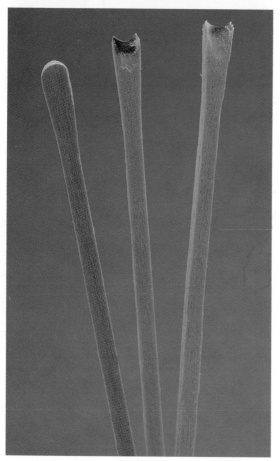

Top left: An easy alternative to carving the toes from wood is to make the complete toe and talon from two-part epoxy putty. Be sure to completely blend the two parts of the epoxy thoroughly. It is helpful to do this under a 60-watt lamp to warm up the epoxy as it is being blended. Once blended, set it aside for about half an hour or so until it begins to firm up. (Several factors will determine the time needed, such as room temperature and how well the putty has been mixed.)

Top right: Once the epoxy has begun firming, take a small amount (about the size of a pea) and roll it on a smooth, flat surface to a diameter of about 3/16 inch, tapering one end to a point. Then gently push on the tapered end, curving it to an arc resembling the curved talon of a kestrel. A small ball of freshly mixed epoxy can now be added to make the fleshy pad found under the front part of the toe.

Left: Tools for embossing in the scales can be easily made by using a large flat toothpick (sold as Craftpiks in most arts and crafts stores) and stoning a curved indentation on the wide end with a 1/8-inch ruby ball run at high speed.

Left: The toes/talons are then placed into position and the ends that attach to the leg shaft are pressed onto it. The putty should still be sticky enough to adhere to the brass. One of the benefits of this technique is that the toes will naturally conform to whatever shape the branch is.

At this point the toes appear to be quite thick, lacking the crisp detail of the actual foot. This is the objective, as the detail and final shape will be stoned in once the putty has fully hardened (usually overnight).

Bottom left: The leg shaft is now wrapped in freshly mixed putty. The leg shape should taper narrower toward the toes. Excess putty is pressed over and around the toes. This will lock it all together once it has hardened.

Bottom right: After 24 hours and careful study of the reference photos, the leg and toes are shaped and detailed. A $1/16$-inch diamond ball works well for the shaping and detailing of the toes and webbing between the toes. Also, a tapered diamond point is useful for shaping and sharpening the underside of the talons.

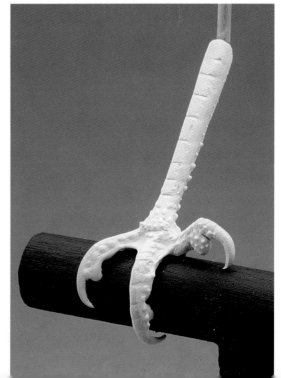

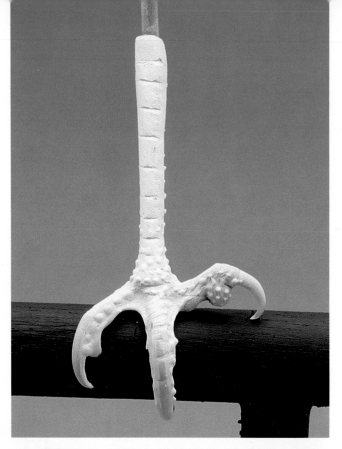

Front view of the foot reveals some additional detailing that can be applied using modeling paste and a pointed brush. This technique is especially useful when creating the many small bumps found throughout the toes and leg, putting forth a "reptilian" look.

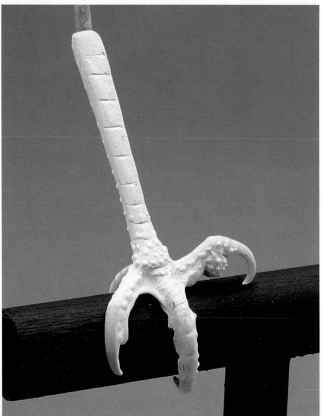

Scale detailing can now be stoned onto the tops of the toes as a final touch.

CHAPTER TEN

Painting and Final Assembly

Of the two disciplines necessary to create a lifelike bird carving, it is the ability, or lack of ability, to paint that will frequently make or break a work. I've seen many mediocre carvings brought to life through skillful painting, but some beautifully carved and textured pieces ruined by a heavy, poorly executed paint job. Taken one step at a time, the American kestrel is not a difficult subject to paint. It is an earthy colored bird with lots of reddish brown coloring. Before beginning the painting process, I attach the kestrel to a holding device to avoid touching the bird and so it is easy to manipulate while I apply the colors.

When choosing a sealer, always use a product that is non-grain-raising and that will penetrate into the wood and not form a film on the surface. Generally, one coat is all that is necessary, but if you know that the work will be displayed in a humid environment or be subjected to extreme shifts in temperature, two coats would be wise. Never spray on sealer, as overspray might leave dry areas and will fuzz up when water-based acrylic paints are applied. After the sealer has thoroughly dried, do not touch the carving. Oil from your hands will prevent the paint from adhering properly to the bird.

Now apply three or four wash coats of gesso mixed to the consistency of skim milk. The objective of gesso is not to turn the bird stark white, but to provide a stable painting base. Strive for consistency; don't overbrush an area. Above all, make sure the first coat is completely dry prior to the next wash, or the gesso will lift and crumble.

When the gesso has dried, the breast, belly, and underside areas are painted a midtone gray color with an airbrush to deepen all the valleys, giving a deep, three-dimensional quality to the surface. The base-tone wash colors are then applied with a 1/2-inch oval wash brush, starting with the rust-colored top of the tail, back, and spot on top of the head. Four to ten washes of this rich color are applied.

Once the base-tone colors have been applied and the shadows are in place, much time is devoted to putting in all the fine detail and plumage markings found throughout the body. My two choices for detail brushes are a number 6 sable and a number 1 sable. If the quality of the brush is excellent, you do not need to use a finer brush than a number 1 sable. Thoroughly clean the eyes after you have finished painting. I'm always surprised at how many artists overlook this detail.

After the paint is dry, the completed feet are epoxied to the tarsus, and a small amount of two-part epoxy putty is used to blend the joints. The bird is now glued to the branch, and the entire work is sprayed with a *very light* spray of clear matte acrylic spray to protect it from the environment. If you are pressed for time and need a quick gap-filling solution for a break or repair, five-minute epoxy can be thickened up with a small amount of talcum powder and colored with a dab of acrylic color.

 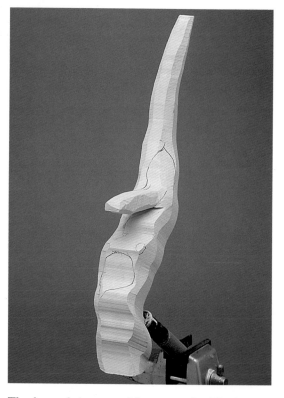

The wood for the base is shown in this picture. One of my favorite woods to use is maple burl because of its beautiful grain and unique properties. The upper portion of this base is maple, and the lower portion is redwood burl. The colors of these woods will complement the finished kestrel.

The branch is carved from tupelo. The band saw is an excellent tool for rough-shaping pieces like this. If necessary, a reinforcing wire may be placed in the protruding branch on which the bird will perch.

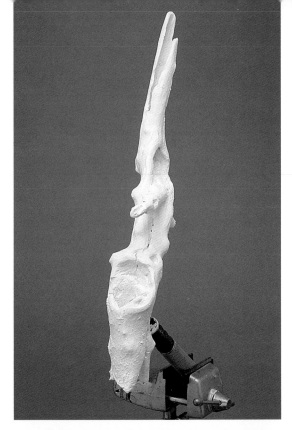

Top left: The branch, after being carved and textured, is ready to be gessoed. A handy item is the holding device pictured, which allows you to paint the branch without touching it. The gesso is applied very thickly, and fine texture is stippled onto the surface as the gesso begins to dry. It is now ready to receive paint.

Top right: The entire composition is now in place. This is an exciting time in the process, as all of the elements are now coming together. The leg shafts are pieces of 1/8-inch brass rod. Balance is very important.

Left: This is the sealer I use for my carvings. It penetrates into the wood and stabilizes it, providing an exceptional surface on which to apply gesso. The sealer is applied with a 1/2-inch oval wash brush.

It's extremely important that you brush on the sealer and not spray it, as your objective is to ensure complete and total coverage. If the bird will be displayed in a damp or humid environment, you may want to apply two coats. After the sealer is applied, do not touch the bird, because oil from your hands will prevent the acrylic paint from adhering properly.

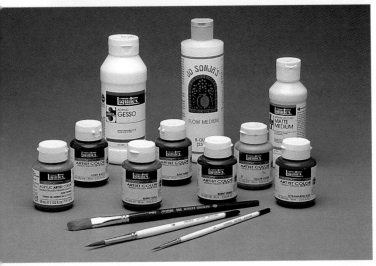

This is my preferred combination of paints. Which brand to use is a matter of personal preference. Be careful, and be aware that colors differ dramatically among manufacturers. The Liquitex jars pictured have convenient snap caps that allow for one-handed opening. I've had very good experience with these paints. I use gesso in place of manufactured whites. Flow medium is helpful in improving the viscosity of the paint as it is mixed and applied to the surface of the carving. A drop or two is all that's needed. Do not use it as a replacement for water.

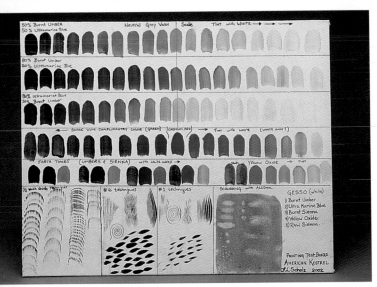

I highly recommend taking the time to preplan all of your color mixes prior to applying them to the bird. A lot can be learned from blending colors and creating a series of value scales using a limited palate of colors. Keep this and refer to it often. It is also helpful to practice brushstrokes and technique to build confidence in your painting ability. I'm always surprised to learn that very little time is devoted to learning to use a brush correctly. Typically, it is not until the carving is completed that any thought is given to painting.

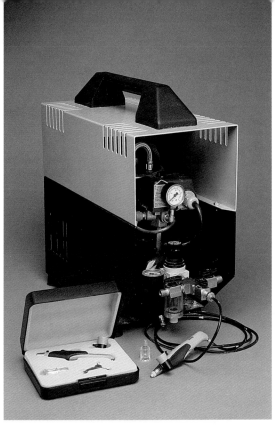

Left: A top-quality compressor is beneficial when airbrushing. I prefer the Aztek Airbrush Set model A4702, available from Jaymes Company (see Appendix). The benefit of this system is the replaceable tips, which are easy to clean and readily available.

Bottom left: Mixing 80 percent raw umber and 20 percent ultramarine blue, apply this mix to the branch with a 1-inch oval wash brush in very thin, watery wash coats. Allow each coat to completely dry before painting the next. Continue applying successive coats until you have achieved the darkness you want.

Bottom right: Another view of the painted branch shows how the pigment settles into the cracks and splits of the painted branch, creating strong contrast.

Top left: Gesso is applied to the bird using a $1/2$-inch oval wash brush. Keep the gesso the consistency of skim milk. The objective is not to turn the bird bright white, but to provide a consistent and balanced surface on which to apply the paint. Four coats should do the trick. Note that the stoned texture will be much brighter white than the burned areas. The gesso can also be applied a bit thicker to the stoned areas, because the texture is not as fine as that of the burned areas.

Top right: A midtone gray mixture of 30 percent burnt umber, 30 percent ultramarine blue, and 40 percent white is airbrushed into all the valleys and used to block in the darker areas found throughout the kestrel's body. Here the airbrush can be a valuable tool. This is what I refer to as monochromatic underpainting. It will show through the top layers of paint, providing a subtle yet important illusion of depth and three-dimensionality.

Left: The front view shows the effectiveness of this process. The bird is now ready for the application of color.

Top left: The rust-colored areas of the back, top of the head, and top of the tail are now being covered with a wash coat of 80 percent burnt sienna, 10 percent burnt umber, and 10 percent yellow oxide. A 1/2-inch oval wash brush is used for this process.

Top right: Six very thin wash coats were applied to achieve the final value and intensity desired. Note how the shadowing effect is evident in this picture. The texturing throughout the back is amplified due to the thinness of the wash coat application.

Left: It can be very helpful to have a test board available to experiment on when you are mixing colors prior to applying them to the surface of the bird. This board is a 1/8-inch-thick piece of tempered masonite with five coats of gesso applied. Make notes on the board so that you can refer back to this handy reference in the future. It illustrates the deepening effect of applying several wash coats.

Top left: The deep blue areas are now painted on using a mixture of 80 percent ultramarine blue, 10 percent raw umber, and 10 percent gesso. They are applied in the same manner as the rust coloring.

Top right: A mixture of 70 percent burnt umber and 30 percent ultramarine blue is used to paint the primaries and darken the vertical markings found around the head. The subterminal band, which spans 3/4 inch, is also painted with this mixture.

Left: Another view of the painted areas. At this point, using straight gesso full strength, the beak and cere are painted white in preparation for their final coloring.

Left: Now 80 percent gesso is mixed with 20 percent Payne's gray and applied to the beak area, covering all the areas beneath the cere. Two to three coats of this mixture will be necessary to provide a consistent covering.

Bottom left: The dark blue tip of the beak is airbrushed using a mixture of 90 percent Payne's gray and 10 percent raw umber. Dampening the surface of the beak prior to airbrushing on the darker color allows a more subtle blending of the two colors.

Bottom right: The cere and eye ring are painted with a mixture of 80 percent yellow oxide and 20 percent gesso. This muted yellow color is applied in three wash coats. The beak is then coated with two layers of satin polyurethane. Do not apply the polyurethane to the cere area. The separation between upper and lower mandibles is carefully painted in with a number 1 sable brush, using a mixture of 90 percent raw umber and 10 percent yellow oxide. (Caution: It is advisable to lay off the coffee prior to this procedure.)

Top left: The dark markings on the back feathers are now painted with a mixture of 50 percent burnt umber and 50 percent ultramarine blue. Pay close attention to your references to ensure accuracy, proper shape, and proper placement of the numerous dark bars and spade-shaped markings. Gradually build the intensity of the dark markings by applying several thin layers.

Top right: The primary feathers, tertials, and upper ends of the secondary covert feathers are delineated with a mixture of 80 percent gesso and 20 percent raw umber. Never apply straight white to a feather edge, as it will look painted. This edging is built up with multiple layers. A number 1 brush was used for this process.

Left: Careful brushwork will enable you to highlight the ridges of the texture lines, creating a soft, featherlike edge on these feather groups. This process "cleans up" a feather group and creates the illusion of feather overlap and directional flow.

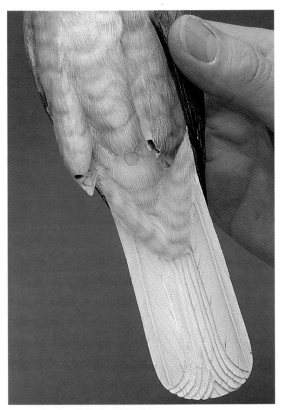

Left: The hole where the holding stick was placed is plugged with two-part epoxy putty. The white regions between the legs and the undertail coverts were first washed with a soft gray color, then the white highlights were put on with a number 1 brush to create the illusion of soft, flowing feathers. The undertail feathers have received four wash coats of white in preparation for the dark, distinctive markings.

Bottom left: A mixture of 50 percent burnt umber and 50 percent ultramarine blue with a touch of flow medium is used in conjunction with a number 6 sable brush to accurately paint in the distinctive markings found on the underside of the tail feathers. It took three applications of color to achieve the final darkness.

Bottom right: Mixing an equal amount of white into the previous mixture results in a soft gray color. This is used to carefully paint in splits in the various feathers. This little bit of extra effort goes a long way in creating an illusion of depth and softness.

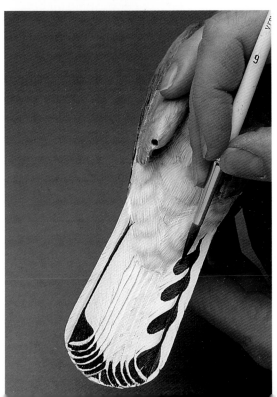

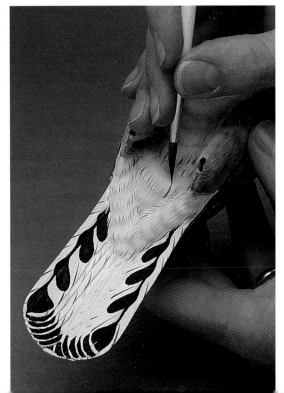

Top left: Using a mixture of 50 percent burnt umber and 50 percent ultramarine blue and a number 6 sable brush, the distinctive spots and spade-shaped markings are painted in along the flanks and up onto the chest area. Be sure to paint the smallest spots on the chest and gradually increase their size as they flow down toward the legs. Arrange them so that they flow and do not appear like polka dots.

Top right: Once the black spots are in place, a number 1 sable brush is used to drag hairlike lines on the spots. This creates the illusion of overlap and translucency in this rather complex area. The color used for these lines is 90 percent gesso and 10 percent raw sienna.

Left: This same mixture is used to highlight areas of feather overlap that occur throughout the upper wrist area and onto the neck. By increasing the amount of flow medium, you will be able to do more painting without needing to go back and recharge your brush.

Top left: Always strive for clean, crisp definition and flow when highlighting overlapping feather groups. This can be very effective in conveying a sense of softness, provided that you stagger the length of the lines.

Top right: Pure white gesso is used with a number 1 sable brush to go back and accentuate the white patches found on the sides of the head. This area cries out for extra brushwork.

Right: Final detailing, such as splits and shadows, is painted in with black paint. The fine tip of a good quality number 1 sable brush is essential in putting in this type of micro detailing. Don't overdue this, because if a bird has too many splits and breaks in its feathers, it is an indication that the bird is sick. This same process can be used for the spots on the flanks.

Top left: Final detailing where the tarsus feathering overlaps the leg is painted in with 90 percent gesso and 10 percent burnt sienna. These areas must not be overlooked. When rendered accurately and creatively, these regions add a tremendous amount to the overall visual appeal of the sculpture. All too often feet and legs are seen as an afterthought and, as a result, detract from the realism of the carving.

Top right: Two-part epoxy putty was used to blend the branch onto the base, creating the illusion that the branch was carved from the base. This can be a very effective transition area. The trick is to match the texture and color of the joint to the completed branch, creating a seamless transition.

Left: As a finishing touch and to add a bit of protection, the overall sculpture is sprayed with a *very light* mist of acrylic matte spray. This will protect your hard work from accumulated dust and airborne debris. Some sprays contain a UV block, which will prevent any fading of colors when exposed to prolonged periods of sunlight.

The Finished Carving

This three-quarters back view reveals the collective effort put into the carving, texturing, and painting. Each discipline should be rendered with the next process in mind. For example: Careful sanding will result in a more consistent and satisfying texture, which in turn provides a better surface upon which to apply paint. The detail work necessary to complete a bird like the American kestrel is something that must not be overlooked. The real trick is in knowing when to stop.

A great deal of time was spent putting in a multitude of fine lines throughout the chest, breast, and belly regions. Collectively, this adds up to an effect of ultimate realism, which is the goal.

This close-up reveals the harmony of a surface area that has been subtly textured with painting in mind. Of particular note is the well-planned flow of feathers up and around the eye and the clean feathering that can be found on the upper wing region.

An overall view of the completed bird. Regardless of how well the artist can carve and paint a bird, if it is not in balance, the entire work will be a failure. Correct foot placement is critical in achieving lifelike balance and harmony throughout the sculpture.

This shows the completed sculpture. The coloring of the base and subbase was no accident. It reflects the rich rust tones found throughout the back of the kestrel. Color balance and harmony are as important as physical balance and harmony in order for the work to be visually dynamic.

List of Suppliers and Related Materials

WOOD AND CARVING SUPPLIES

Brad Ketrick
4928 Timber Green Lane
Holly Springs, NC 27540
919-612-8777

Buck Run Carving Supplies
30 Wheeler Street
Hancock, NY 13783
800-438-6807

Christian J. Hummul Co.
P.O. Box 522
Nescopeck, PA 18635-0522
800-762-0235

Curt's Waterfowl Corner
4033 Country Drive
Bourg, LA 70343
800-523-8474 (orders)
985-580-3014

Dux Dekes
1356 North Road
Greenwich, NY 12834
800-553-4725
518-692-7703
www.duxdekes.com
duxdekes@capital.net

Foredom Electric Company
16 Stony Hill Road
Bethel, CT 06801
203-792-8622
203-796-7861 (fax)
www.foredom.com

Gesswein Tool Company
255 Hancock Ave.
Bridgeport, CT 06605
800-544-2043

Jaymes Company
234 Cartland Way
Forest Hill, MD 21050
888-638-8998

Jenning's Decoy Company
601 Franklin Ave. NE
St. Cloud, MN 56304
800-331-5613
320-253-9537 (fax)

Little Mountain Carving Supply
179 Bowling Green Road
Front Royal, VA 22630
540-636-3125

MDI Woodcarvers Supply
228 Main Street
Bar Harbor, ME 04609
info@mdiwoodcarvers.com
800-866-5728

Ritter Carvers, Inc.
640 Bethlehem Pike
Colmar, PA 18915
215-997-3395
800-242-0682 (orders)

Sugar Pine Woodcarving Supplies
800-452-2783
541-451-5455 (fax)

Woods-Work
9725 E. Washington Street
Indianapolis, IN 46229
317-897-4198
317-897-5714 (fax)

GLASS EYES

G. Schoepfer, Inc.
460 Cook Hill Road
Cheshire, CT 06410
800-875-6939

Tohican Glass Eyes
Box 15
15 Geigel Hill Road
Erwinna, PA 18920
800-441-5983

WOODBURNING TOOLS AND EQUIPMENT

Colwood Electronics
15 Meridian Road
Eatontown, NJ 07724
732-544-1119

Detail Master—Leisure Time Products, Inc.
2650 Davisson Street
River Grove, IL 60171
708-452-5400
www.detailmasteronline.com

Hot Tools, Inc.
P.O. Box 615-V
Marblehead, MA 01945
781-639-1000

Razertip Industries, Inc.
P.O. Box 910
Martensville, SK
CANADA S0K 2T0
877-729-3787
306-931-0889
www.razertip.com
razertip@sk.sympatico.ca

DECORATIVE WOOD BASES

Blue Ribbon Bases
100K Knickerbocker Ave.
Bohemia, NY 11716
888-692-9257

Displays by Rioux
P.O. Box 3008
Syracuse, NY 13220-3008
888-327-4689
315-458-3722
displaysbyrioux@att.net
www.displaysbyrioux.com

WOODS FOR MAKING BASES

Burlwood, Inc., Exotic Hardwoods
c/o Lorin Sandberg
41015 Larwood Drive
Scio, OR 97374
503-394-3077
www.burlwoodonline.com

PAINTING AND AIRBRUSH SUPPLIES

BearAir Express
800-232-7247
www.bearair.com

Black Horse Artists Supply
200 Main Street
Burlington, VT 05401
800-790-2552

STUDY CASTS

Waterfowl Study Bills, Inc.
P.O. Box 310
Evergreen, LA 71333
318-346-4814
318-346-7633 (fax)

PUBLICATIONS

Birder's World Magazine
800-533-6644
www.birdersworld.com

Chip Chats
7424 Miami Ave.
Cincinnati, OH 45243
513-561-0627
nwca@chipchats.org
www.chipchats.org

Stackpole Books
5067 Ritter Road
Mechanicsburg, PA 17055-6921
800-732-3669

WildBird Magazine
WildBird Subscription Department
P.O. Box 52898
Boulder, CO 80322-2898
800-365-4421

Wildfowl Carving Magazine
1300 Market Street, Ste. 202
Lemoyne, PA 17043-1420
wcc@paonline.com
www.wildfowl-carving.com
717-234-1359 (fax)

ORGANIZATIONS

National Audubon Society
800-274-4201
audubon@neodata.com
www.audubon.org

Raptor Trust of New Jersey
1390 White Bridge Road
Millington, NJ 07946
908-647-2353

World Center for Birds of Prey
5666 W. Flying Hawk Lane
Boise, ID 83709
208-362-3716

WOODWORKING MACHINERY, BAND SAWS

Delta International Machinery
246 Alpha Drive
Pittsburgh, PA 15238
800-438-2486
www.deltawoodworking.com

Jet Equipment & Tools
P.O. Box 1349
Auburn, WA 98071-1349
800-274-6848
www.jettools.com

Lenox
American Saw & Manufacturing Company
301 Chestnut Street
East Longmeadow, MA 01028
800-628-3030
www.lenoxsaw.com

Powermatic
619 Morrison Street
McMinnville, TN 37110
800-248-0144
www.powermatic.com